YOU CHOOSE BOOKS™

P9-BYJ-292

AT BATTLE IN THE CIVIL WAR

AN INTERACTIVE BATTLEFIELD ADVENTURE

by Allison Lassieur

Consultant:
James McPherson
Professor of American History, Emeritus
Princeton University, Princeton, New Jersey

CAPSTONE PRESS
a capstone imprint

You Choose Books are published by Capstone Press,
1710 Roe Crest Drive, North Mankato, Minnesota 56003
www.capstonepub.com

Library of Congress Cataloging-in-Publication Data
Lassieur, Allison.
  At battle in the Civil War : an interactive battlefield adventure / by Allison Lassieur.
    pages cm. — (You choose books. You choose: battlefields.)
  Summary: "In You Choose format, explores the Civil War from the view of infantry,
artillery, and cavalry soldiers"—Provided by publisher.
  Includes bibliographical references and index.
  ISBN 978-1-4914-2149-9 (library binding)
  ISBN 978-1-4914-2391-2 (paperback)
  ISBN 978-1-4914-2395-0 (eBook PDF)
1. United States—History—Civil War, 1861–1865—Juvenile literature. 2. Soldiers—
United States—History—19th century—Juvenile literature. 3. Soldiers—Confederate
States of America—Juvenile literature. I. Title.
  E468.L27 2015
  973.7—dc23   2014023840

Editorial Credits

Mari Bolte, editor; Tracy Davies McCabe and Charmaine Whitman, designers;
Wanda Winch, media researcher; Laura Manthe, production specialist

Photo Credits

(Clubs are Trumps) by Dale Gallon, Courtesy of Gallon Historical Art,
www.gallon.com, cover, (The Hornets' Nest) by Dale Gallon, Courtesy of Gallon
Historical Art, www.gallon.com, 45; Bear River Homestead: James Martin, 23;
Bridgeman Images/Private Collection/Robert Marshall Root, 6; Corbis: Bettmann,
15, ©Medford Historical Society Collection, 8, 91; CriaImages.com: Jay Robert Nash
Collection, 30–31, 42, 73, 84, 102; Getty Images: Hulton Archive/Three Lions,
21, MPI, 88; James P. Rowan, 52, 66; Library of Congress: Prints and Photographs
Division, 27, 48, 55, 61, 64, 100; National Archives and Records Administration, 12,
70; North Wind Picture Archives, 10, 36; www.historicalimagebank.com, Painting by
Don Troiani, 78, 98

Printed in Canada.
092014   008478FRS15